THE GATE IS ON
BACKWARDS

GLEN WATTS

ILLUSTRATIONS BY CATALINA SAN ROMÁN MUÑOZ

The Gate Is On Backwards

Copyright © 2025 by Glen Watts.

MILTON & HUGO L.L.C.
4407 Park Ave., Suite 5
Union City, NJ 07087, USA

Website: www. miltonandhugo.com
Hotline: 1- 888-778-0033
Email: info@miltonandhugo.com

Ordering Information:
Quantity sales. Special discounts are available on quantity purchases by corporations, associations, and others. For details, contact the publisher at the address above.

Library of Congress Control Number: 2024924382
ISBN-13:   979-8-89285-365-1   [Paperback Edition]
             979-8-89285-366-8   [Hardback Edition]
             979-8-89285-364-4   [Digital Edition]

Rev. date: 04/21/2025

THE GATE IS ON
BACKWARDS

FOR MOM
AND
FOR DAD

BY GLEN WATTS
ILLUSTRATIONS BY CATALINA SAN ROMÁN MUÑOZ

There's a gate at the
end of our drive

With rusty hinges, a chain, and a pin

Seems to me it doesn't
swing the right way

It turns out, when
it ought to turn in

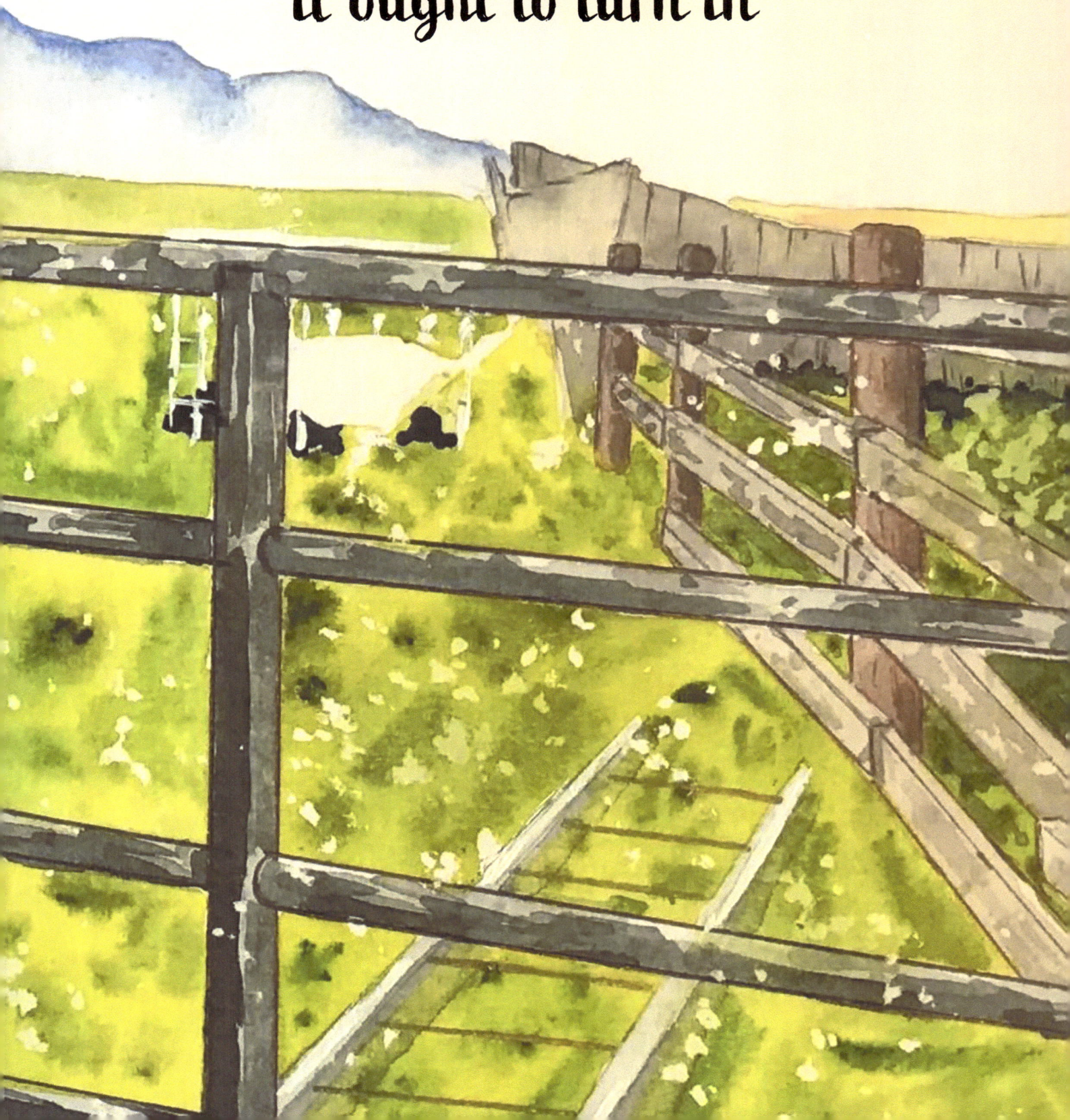

It's been there as long as I know,
on backwards from how it should go

I don't really know why,
but I'm sure that I'm right,

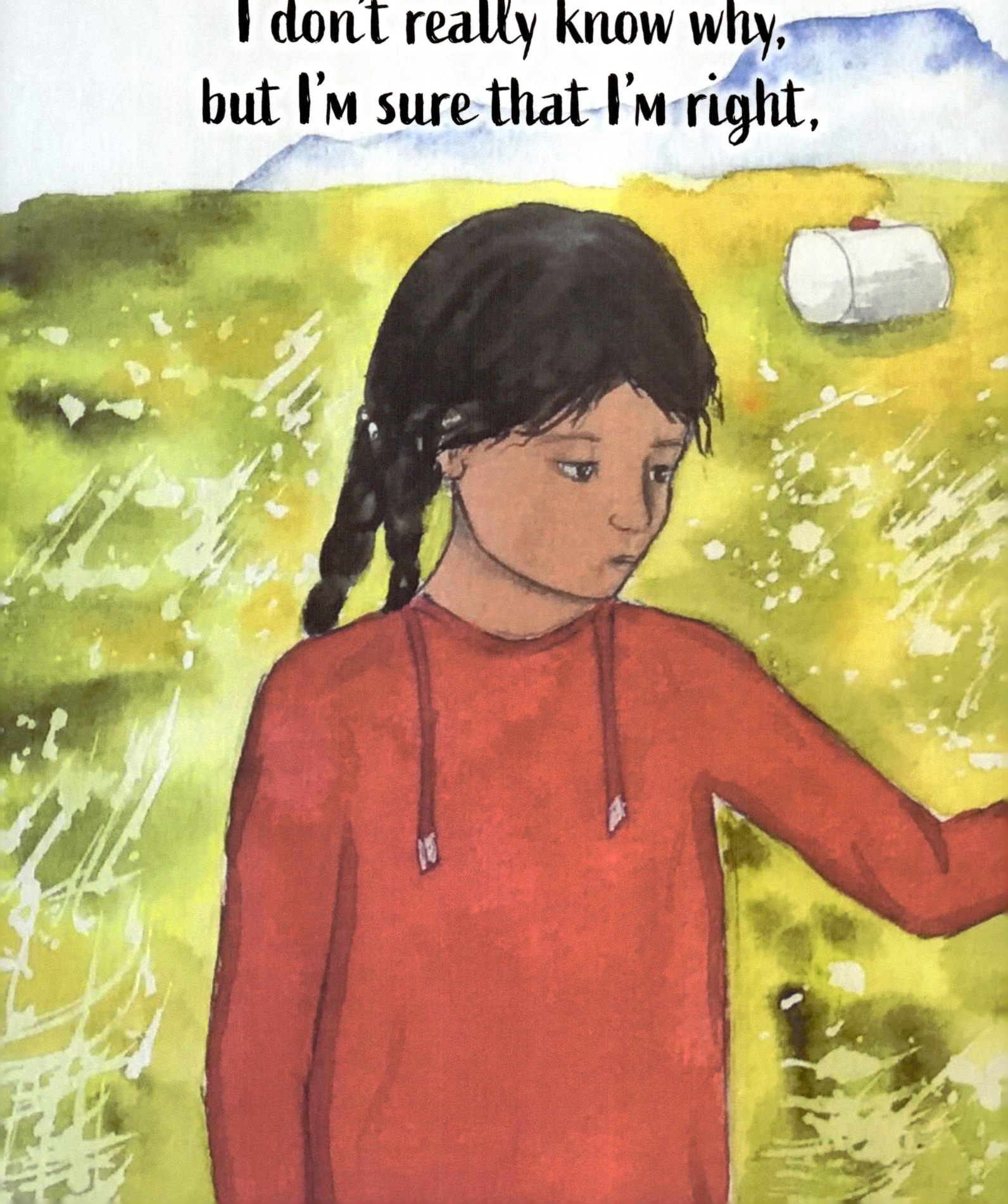

'bout this gate at
the end of our drive

"The gate is on backwards." I said to my mom. "Turns out, but it ought to turn in."

"Go talk to your father." She said licking her thumb and then rubbing some dirt off my chin

"The gate is on backwards." I said to my dad. "The hinges don't swing the right way."

"What makes you say that!?" He scowled, and then I suddenly had nothing to say

"The gate is on backwards."
I said to my sister

"Come here, and I'll show you right now!"

"What goes on in your head, anyhow?"

"The gate is on backwards, Grandpa."

I sighed.

"... Yep ..."

"Never could explain it to your grandma, though."

Then, he
sighed too.

www.ingramcontent.com/pod-product-compliance
Lightning Source LLC
Chambersburg PA
CBHW060813090426

42737CB00002B/52